USBORNE BIBLE TALES
DAVID & GOLIATH

Retold by Heather Amery

Illustrated by Norman Young
Designed by Maria Wheatley

Language consultant: Betty Root
Series editor: Jenny Tyler

This is David.

He lived a long time ago in Israel. He looked after his father's sheep out on the hills.

David was very brave.

He fought lions and bears which tried to kill the sheep. He thought God kept him safe.

He went to the army camp.

David's father asked him to take food to his three brothers. They were soldiers in King Saul's army.

The two armies watched each other.

King Saul's army looked across the valley. They saw their enemies, the Philistines, on the other side.

One soldier was a giant.

His name was Goliath. He was a huge and very
strong man. He had a spear and a sword.

Every day he shouted a challenge.

"Send one man to fight me," he yelled. But King Saul's soldiers were too scared to go.

"I will fight him," said David.

"You are only a boy," said King Saul. "God has helped me to kill bears and lions," said David.

"You may go," said King Saul.

"But you must wear my fighting clothes." David put
them on but they were much too big and heavy.

David took off the clothes.

He picked up five small stones for his sling. Then he walked across the valley to fight Goliath.

Goliath laughed at him.

"Come here, boy," he said, "and I will kill you."
David said, "God will help me to fight you."

David put a stone in his sling.

He swung it around his head, faster and faster. He let it go and the little stone flew out.

The stone hit Goliath.

It hit the giant right in the middle of his forehead.
He fell down on the ground.

David ran up to Goliath.

The giant lay quite still. David saw that he was dead. The little stone had killed him.

King Saul's army cheered.

The Philistine soldiers were frightened and they ran away. King Saul's army chased them.

David had won.

All the people in Israel were delighted by his victory.
They danced and sang songs about David.

This edition first published in 2004 by Usborne Publishing Ltd, 83-85 Saffron Hill,
London EC1N 8RT, England. www.usborne.com Copyright © 2004, 1996 Usborne Publishing Ltd.
The name Usborne and the devices ♀ ⊕ are Trade Marks of Usborne Publishing Ltd. All rights reserved. No part of this publication may be
reproduced, stored in a retrieval system, or transmitted in any form or by any means, electronic, mechanical, photocopying, recording
or otherwise, without prior permission of the publisher. UE. This edition first published in America in 2004. Printed in China.